My Day at Disney

To all who read

this happy book:

"Welcome!"

My Day at Disney

stories from the disney theme parks told by people just like you and me

COLLECTED BY

BRAD WILLIAMSON

Favorite Son Press
Vancouver, WA

Editor: Jill Williamson

First Printing, 2019
ISBN 978-1-0761319-7-3

Favorite Son Press
Vancouver, WA

This book is dedicated to

AARON CHUMBLEY

Thanks for kickstarting my obsession with Disneyland!

"Welcome, Foolish Mortals!"

Disney is full of stories and history. Walt would come up with an idea, share it with his team of creative geniuses, and it would grow into something magical. *Steamboat Willie* led to the cartoon shorts. *Snow White and the Seven Dwarfs* led to the animated features. And of course, Disneyland led to the theme parks. The Disney parks have their own history, just like Mickey Mouse and Snow White.

I consider myself to be a professional, amateur Disney historian. I read articles and watch YouTube videos frequently just so I can learn more about Walt and his empire. I love Disneyland history, but I get tired of reading the same trivia and the same stories again and again. Maybe you understand what I'm talking about...

Let's test this with a quick quiz:
1) What household animal roams around Disneyland each night?
2) What sport can be played inside the Matterhorn?
3) Where can you find a sign from the old Eeyore parking lot?
4) Where is Walt's Disneyland apartment located?
5) How many times has the drawbridge been raised on Sleeping Beauty's castle?

If you were able to answer all of those questions without thinking, then you have the same problem as me... You need new stories! That's what this book is about. New stories from new voices. Voices just like yours and mine. Voices that have never had the chance to tell their stories because they don't have a last name like Disney, Sklar, or Sherman. But the stories you'll find in this book are just as fascinating. These are the stories that come from the tourists. These stories come from YOU!

I am the guy who could spend a whole day at a Disney park and love every minute of it, even if I never got on a ride. Open to close is the ONLY way to enjoy the parks! Every person there comes in with their own story, their own expectation based on what Disney means to them, from the toddler who is excited just to meet Mickey Mouse to the older adult who remembers being terrified by the giant eye at the end of Adventure Thru Inner Space.

Some of the greatest memories I have come from Disneyland, but I can't quite put my finger on what they are. I have a distinct recollection of walking past the entrance to critter country and hearing Rufus the Bear snoring in a cave somewhere above me. I remember walking through Tomorrowland and watching as three garbage collectors paused in the middle of the walkway and started playing their garbage cans like drums. I recall sitting on my dad's lap on Space Mountain and being too afraid to open my eyes during the entire pitch-black ride! All of these are just little blips and images, but they all come from my favorite place in the world: Disneyland.

I grew up on the west coast, so I was a Disneyland kid. Many of you reading this are Walt Disney World kids. Or maybe you've even done a Disney cruise. All of them are amazing, and all of them are magical! No matter which park is your favorite, they are all full of stories and full of memories. This book was written to preserve those memories and let us all go back to the parks together. You might read something familiar in here or something that reminds you of an interesting day you had at a Disney park. And I really hope you do.

Disney set a new standard for how a theme park should operate: clean, friendly, and fun. Walt Disney envisioned a place where parents and kids could have fun together in an environment that was safe and inviting. And it worked! Since 1955, Disney parks have entertained billions of people from every country on the globe. Families from different ethnicities, religions, social classes, and political views have all come together to visit The Happiest Places on Earth.

This book is for them: the people who love Disney so much, they save up for the whole year to buy a ticket, the people who buy season passes and go every afternoon, and the people who went once and the experience has lived on in their minds forever.

I have asked family, friends, and complete strangers (just say "Howdy, stranger!") for their stories from Disney so we could relive the magic together. The stories you'll find in these pages are their own stories in their own words. So come along and sing the song. If you really feeling saucy, go ahead and join the jamboree. Let's go spend a Day at Disney!

-Brad Williamson

P.S. Here are the answers to the quiz:
1) Cats. 2) Basketball, 3) Indiana Jones ride movie room, 4) Above the fire house, 5) Twice

BONUS!

Uh oh! It seems that Peter Pan is not the only one to lose his shadow! For a little bit of extra fun, twenty silhouettes of Disney characters have been added to this book. All the characters shown gained popularity from their role in one of the many Disney parks around the world. Some of them are walk-around characters, and some are audio-animatronics. (You'll also find Mickey Mouse in there somewhere!) See how many of the characters you can figure out from their shadows. Some are pretty easy, but there are a few you might not recognize. The answers can be found at the back of the book.

REMAIN SEATED, PLEASE...
PERMANECER SENTADOS,
POR FAVOR.

Aaron

I went with my friend and her family to Disneyland in 1984. We were both about the same size and the same age, about 9 years old, so we rode most of the rides together. At this time, the Rocket Jets were located on top of the People Mover platform, high above Tomorrowland.

Like always, the two of us went to ride the Rocket Jets together. So we get up, it's our turn and the cast member says to us, "Okay, you guys go ahead and get in." He points to my friend and says, "You go in front," then points at me, "and you go on the back." We step up to the rocket, my friend gets in the front seat, and I got on the back. On the back! Not in the back seat or sitting behind her, but I literally thought he meant sit on the back of the rocket.

So I did.

I straddled the rocket. The fin of the rocket was pushing against my rear end. He didn't say anything. He didn't check anything. I literally thought I had done what he said to do. Of course, in hindsight I realized he wanted me to sit behind my friend in the seat, but I didn't realize that at the time.

And off we went.

The ride started up and I'm straddling this rocket. I freaked out! I was terrified that I was going to fall off. We were way up high already but the rockets went even higher. I don't think I would have fallen all the way

to the ground, but even the People Mover platform would have been far enough.

I'm screaming at my friend who was holding the control stick that made the rocket go up and down, "You have to go low! Don't go high! Don't go high! You have to keep it low! Keep it low!" They didn't stop it; they didn't do anything. I rode on the back of the rocket until the ride was over, and then I got off and that was that. Nobody ever said a word.

Abby and Pluto

Abby

I grew up in a small town in South Dakota. When I was about seven years old in 1991, I went to my uncle's wedding in California. Like most kids, I was a Disney girl. The rerelease of *101 Dalmatians* was the first movie I saw in the theater. But I didn't know what Disneyland was, or what to expect.

I was the youngest of my family, and I was scared of the rides. They assured me that these weren't scary. It was Disneyland! They would be cute! The first ride we went on was Thunder Mountain Railroad. As an adult that ride isn't scary but as a seven-year-old-I remember barley being able to hold my head up as it took one turn after another. After we got off that ride, my family told me they would take it easy and go on slower rides. We walked through Tarzan's Treehouse, took a jungle cruise, and then we went on Pirates of the Caribbean... after the second drop, I had it! My family lied to me! Disneyland is scary!!! I remember getting off the boat in tears.

My Dad agreed to stay with me while the others went their own way. He wasn't feeling well, and I wasn't going to be fooled into going on a scary ride again! I spent the rest of my day with my puking father, alone on rides. I burst into tears sitting in a tea cup by myself, not being strong enough to make it spin. I was done with Disneyland. What was so magical about this place?

Standing outside the thirteenth men's room for the day, I had my arms folded and my pouty face on. I was ready to go home. Then Pluto came

dancing up to me and tried to make me smile. I showed him nothing was going to shake my funk. Dad came out of the bathroom to see Pluto dancing. He took a photo of us and Pluto waved us to follow him into a restaurant. We walked with Pluto into the restaurant where a whole slew of characters were getting ready to go "on stage." I arm wrestled with Captain Hook and learned to "fly" with Peter Pan, it was magical! Pluto gave me a big hug before he left and patted me on the head.

My heart was full! After that, Dad bought me a pair of Minnie Mouse ears and a glass full of strawberry candy with a Minnie Mouse lid. I still have my ears, which I refurbished and mounted for display in my office.

Sixteen years later, I am getting married to the love of my life and he says, "Let's honeymoon at Disneyland!" I shook my head! No way! That place was kind of awful! He eventually talked me into giving it another shot so he could help erase any bad memories! We spun so fast on the Tea Cups that I laughed all the bad memories away! We had a blast. We ended up in Toon Town where I ran into Pluto. He patted me on the head and in an instant, I burst into happy tears. Pluto had been my savior when I was seven, and that familiar pat brought back a rush of emotion.

To this day I am an avid Disneyland fan. I go with friends, with myself, and with family, and I ALWAYS make time to say hello to Pluto!

WHO HAS LOST THEIR SHADOW?

Adrienne

In May of 2017 I was blessed with the opportunity to go to Orlando to work at a conference, and to my great joy and excitement, I was able to go down a day early for a grand Disney Day all to myself. I went to Hollywood Studios, my favorite park, and I remember getting off the bus and being overwhelmed to the point of tears. I couldn't believe that I was here for the second time in my life at just twenty-one years old, when all my childhood it had seemed impossible to go even once.

I had an amazing time that day, getting to ride The Great Movie Ride for what would be the last time (RIP Great Movie Ride — you were the best), met a charming boy from Europe in the single rider line of Rockin' Roller Coaster, and helped a lost child find a cast member to help him locate his tour group.

The day was magic, and to top it off, I was going to have lunch at 50s Prime Time Cafe—a huge treat that I was giving myself because it was my birthday weekend and I love everything to do with the 50s!

I was seated next to a large family, and we ended up chatting a bit. We found out that we were from the same town, and had similar lifestyles. They were extremely kind and fun to talk to. When I had finished my meal, my server was taking a very long time to get my check to me. I was starting to get a little antsy. When he finally arrived, he told me that I was good to go—the family had paid for my meal!

That is what I love most about Disney. When people who you probably will never meet again go out of their way to be kind and make extra magic for another guest. Whether it's smiling and complimenting someone's handmade Minnie Ears, offering to show you where a ride or restaurant is, or going above and beyond and paying for someone's meal. Kindness is beautiful, and you can find so much of it at Disney.

Poor sick Amberly

Amberly

In February of 2009, I went to Walt Disney World for a week with my best friend for her thirteenth birthday. Just before going, I caught strep throat, the flu, AND had vertigo all at the same time! But, being the determined little twelve-year-old that I was, I fought the illness and got to experience most of Disney World...from a park stroller. You know, those big ones that are designed for families with numerous tiny offspring? The ones meant for toddlers? Yeah, those. Little twelve-year-old me cruised around Disneyworld in that.

I was so embarrassed about that for the longest time, but now it cracks me up whenever I think about it. It's a good reminder for me to be tenacious regardless of how horrible I feel. While I was there, I also got to see my first Cirque du Soleil show! Front row, my feet could touch the stage. Why? Cause the little Amberly-Engine-That-Could fought this deathly illness and made sure I enjoyed my best friend's thirteenth birthday and everything that came with it.

In case you were wondering, I threw up everywhere on the plane ride home and proceeded to be violently ill for the next two weeks after the trip. Not the best ending but, still, lesson learned.

Andrew

My wife and I have a passion for traveling. Our first trip as a couple was to Disneyland Resort and, from that point, Disney Parks became an important piece of our lives. While we love visiting other places throughout the world, going to these theme parks together has always made us happier. Right around the time we got married (and honeymooned at Walt Disney World) I started to read more and more about Disney Parks and one place always stood out – Tokyo DisneySea.

In 2018, after five years of marriage, we had saved enough money and I'd successfully convinced my wife and two of our best friends to take a dream trip to Japan with me. I'd read every guide I could about the country and Tokyo Disney Resort. I dreamed of stepping foot in DisneySea and finally getting a glimpse at the park, instead of just looking at photos. We spent the first few days of our trip in Kyoto, now our favorite city in the world. We explored Tokyo and got lost in its massive skyline and beautiful artistry. Eventually, our trip came to its climactic conclusion with Tokyo Disney Resort.

We arrived late in the afternoon and got a ticket for that evening (along with a four-day ticket following that). After checking into our hotel, we took the monorail from our hotel to DisneySea and walked in the gates. Frankly, that part was a blur. Eventually we stood at the net rope at the front of DisneySea, looking out at the water and Mount Prometheus, the

park's icon. I'd seen that same view in photos over and over for five years, hoping one day that I'd get to see it for myself. With my wife holding my hand and my best friends beside me, I began to cry.

It all seems a bit silly, having one of my main goals and dreams be going to a theme park. There are more meaningful things in life. Then again, I could have stood in that spot for hours, feeling more content than I ever have. My best friends and I set out on an adventure and the journey concluded with a storybook sunset in a place that I dreamed about. It may have been just a few people going to a theme park, but it will forever be more meaningful than that to me.

Andrew's long-awaited view

WHO HAS LOST THEIR SHADOW?

Anne

Sometimes children love the idea of Disneyland more than the park itself. We took our girls to Disneyland in summer of 1997. We're from the Pacific Northwest and my two-year-old daughter, Kirsten, was not a fan of the California heat. We would attempt to meet Mickey and Minnie. We would try to take her on rides. We would struggle to get her a snack. Each time she would show her excitement by saying, "It's too hot!" or "Can we go back to the hotel?" Eventually we gave up and went back to our hotel room.

That's where she really got into the Disney experience.

We were exhausted from dealing with a grumpy child, but she was full of energy. She asked if we wanted to see a show. She jumped on the bed shouting, "I'm Meeko!" Then she would lean forward and change the pretend channel on a pretend TV. "Now, I'm Pocahontas!" Jump jump jump. She'd change the channel again. "Now I'm Flit!" She went through so many of them: Cinderella, Quasimodo, Esmerelda..." It was pretty adorable.

When the sun went down, we returned to the park and Kirsten was a whole new girl. She was laughing and happy. That night, when the Light Magic Parade started, she was chosen to march along with the Cast Members. She danced and giggled her way through part of the parade.

After all of her whining and complaining, she still ended up having the best time a two-year-old can have. She missed half the day in the park, but she still has nothing but fond memories of her day at Disneyland!

Ellie with Buzz and Woody

Ashley P.

We brought our daughter Ellie on her first trip to Walt Disney World in 2017. She was very young, just barely two-years-old, and we were worried that she would freak out when meeting the characters. She seemed so excited, but you just never know how a child will react when they come face to face with giant versions of their favorite cartoon celebrities, especially Buzz and Woody. They were her favorite at the time. We were fully prepared by the time we got to Hollywood Studios. We re-watched all three movies and the made-for-TV specials about five times on the way there.

The moment finally came. Our very first character meet-up was with Buzz and Woody and Ellie was even wearing her Woody costume! I'm proud to say that she absolutely loved it! She was grinning from ear to ear, and the smile never left her face the entire trip!

Ashley's complete collection

Ashley T.

Ever since I learned about Disney pin trading, I was hooked! My brother and I are obsessive traders. We look for pin collections we like and hunt for the whole collection. When we were at Disney World in 2011, I was eight years old and thought it would be fun to collect all the Disney pin letters of my name to put on the cover of my pin trading album. A-H-L-E-Y were pretty easy to find, so I had collected them by the second day of the trip. But as the week went on I just couldn't find the letter "S." I had my whole extended family looking for an "S" pin to complete my name.

We were at Epcot the last day of our trip and I had really hoped that Epcot Pin Central would have an "S." Total disappointment... no "S." My cousin and I were just coming off the Fast Track ride when my brother sent me a text that I needed to come to Ellen's Energy Adventure right away! I totally thought something was wrong because he didn't say why I needed to go there. He only said, "Just hurry." My cousin and I ran to the Ellen ride and found my brother with a Disney cast member. I noticed right away that the cast member was wearing trading pins and sure enough, she had an "S!"

I was so happy that I lost my mind and gave my brother the biggest bear hug right in the middle of Epcot. It wasn't until I opened my eyes and saw the sheer terror on my brother's face that I realized what I had done. We have never talked about that hug since.

DISNEY PARKS
AROUND THE WORLD

Disneyland – 1955

Magic Kingdom – 1971

Epcot – 1982

Tokyo Disneyland – 1983

Disney's Hollywood Studios – 1989

Disneyland Paris – 1992

Disney's Animal Kingdom – 1998

Disney's California Adventure – 2001

Tokyo DisneySea - 2001

Walt Disney Studios Park – 2005

Shanghai Disneyland – 2018

Barb

On May 4, 2005, Disneyland was closed to the public. It's extremely rare for Disneyland to be closed for a whole day since the park went to a seven-day operating week. But, in celebration of their 50th anniversary, Disneyland held a media day where only members of various press outlets and special guests were invited. I was selected as an annual passholder to attend and see all of the decorations ahead of most people. Coincidentally, it was also my 50th year! It was very magical.

We were there all day from before sunup to after sundown. Although the park was closed to the general public, it was still very crowded. We waited with many other annual pass holders in California Adventure for several hours in order to get into the park. When we finally got in, there was a red carpet and the cast were all there greeting us.

They gave away free cupcakes. If you were crazy enough, like me, you could wait in line for a few hours to get day-of merchandise. I got my merchandise, but I also got a sunburn! If you were like my friend, you could wait a few days and get the same things on eBay.

All of the original rides had one conveyance that was painted gold in celebration of the golden anniversary. They remained that way for the rest of the anniversary year. Richard Sherman and Art Linkletter were there, and I got to meet both of them. It was truly a magical day, and it felt like Walt was there watching!

WHO HAS LOST THEIR SHADOW?

Becky E.

Frequent visits to Disneyland were part of my childhood growing up in Southern California, so by the time our senior class held its all-night grad party at Disneyland in 1967, I had been on all the rides numerous times. It's hard to admit, but I may have been too tired that night to fully enjoy it.

My boyfriend and I had been to our senior prom plus a church party earlier that week, so after just a few rides at Disneyland, we agreed that we were too tired to keep going. We decided to find a place we could rest for a while. We hopped on the Disneyland Railroad that circles the entire theme park, closed our eyes and fell asleep. To this day, we have no idea how many times the train went around! At some point, we finally woke up and got off.

It doesn't seem like it would be possible, but yes, a teenager can actually fall asleep at the Magic Kingdom! The Disney magic still worked out though... I married that boyfriend, and I'm still with him 50 years later!

Becky H.

It was my sister's senior year, and I was ten when we went to Disney. An annual trip for our family. Hollywood Studios was called Disney-MGM back then, and it was my favorite because it was a show park. The Beauty and the Beast show was magical.

There was a gameshow that trip. The audience was waiting in an outdoor atrium when a host stood on stage and asked for volunteers. I can't recall what he said or if he had jokes or banter as he selected people out of the audience. I'm sure he picked people by gender and age. My mom volunteered me. I was a shy kid! I loved being on stage in theater, but auditioning was frightening!

The host cast member handed me a slip of paper and pointed me backstage. Another cast member excitedly sent me to my seat! I remember my sister being backstage also. We were all in groups of three or four, and we were given some costumes or costume pieces.

Once we were all selected, the rest of the audience was seated in an indoor theater where they were treated to a show of their fellow Disney tourists! They had a moving set with different scenes and backgrounds. There were television screens backstage where we could watch the show.

I saw my sister — she had been grouped in a girl singing trio. The three girls were dressed in red glittery sequin dresses and had to act out a Supremes hit.

It was my turn! My group had *Gilligan's Island*. I was Mrs. Howell. A cast member handed me some fake money to wave. A guy was cycling on a stationary bike as Gilligan. The movie star had to blow kisses. Someone was the Professor. Our little fake island rotated on the turntable and the spotlight hit us... the audience cheered... we were "stars" for a few minutes! And then we were turned back to the dark of the backstage. Ushered out of our costumes and back out to the sunlight to our families and on our way.

It was so fun! It was a show that didn't last though. My family went yearly, and that's the only time I ever recall doing that. I think maybe we watched it once but weren't selected. I'm fairly certain it was replaced by The *Who Wants to Be a Millionaire* show. I think it would be refreshing to see it come back one day. Give others a chance at stardom. Everyone loves a little fame!

Bella's honeymoon photo shoot

BELLA

My all-time favorite Disney memory was on our honeymoon. All I wanted to do the whole time was see Minnie Mouse, so on our second day we stood in line for a good twenty minutes to see her. We were the only adults in line without children.

Minnie was spending about one minute with each kid. When we got to the front, she saw the pins we were wearing that said "Just Married," and she proceeded to spend a good ten-to-fifteen minutes with us! She walked around and made us do a photo shoot with her, completely posing us for each picture herself! Then she took my autograph book and drew us a picture. I'm telling you, it was a huge ordeal! I was twenty and never felt more like a little kid in my life. It was magical. We showed her pictures of our Disney wedding, and she gave us more pins. I was so happy. By the time we were done taking pictures, she had to go, so none of the other kids in line got to meet her. And I couldn't even apologize!

BETH

I have a lot of very fond memories from Walt Disney World. Like when my son was two and Donald Duck spent several minutes teasing him. Taking out his pacifier and then giving back, again and again. It was adorable and my son loved it.

It truly is a magical place, full of wonder and fun, especially if you're a child. But my most vivid memory of MY childhood at Disney World was not exactly magical...

We had spent the whole day in the Magic Kingdom, walking around, going on rides, and seeing the shows. I was ten years old, the perfect age to soak up everything the park had to offer. It was summertime, and the Florida heat was pretty intense, bringing all sorts of critters along with it. It was 1972 and Walt Disney World had been open less than a year, so they had not yet learned how to control certain things... like tics!

It was about one in the morning and the place was completely shut down for the night. We were walking through the mostly empty parking lot to find our car when a custodian stopped us because he noticed a big fat tic on the back of my neck! We stood under one of the lights in the parking lot, and my dad used his lit cigar to burn the tic as they tried to coax it out. When the tic finally loosened its grip, the custodian grabbed it, threw it to the ground, and crushed it under his shoe. The custodian told us to have a good night and went back to his duties.

My parents had recently read of children having serious injuries from tic bites, so they were like, "If you wake up and can't move, let us know." I was like, "Welp, okaaayy...."

I did NOT suffer any complications from my ordeal, and now, years later, I love taking my own children to Walt Disney's Magic Kingdom, tic free, of course!

WHO HAS LOST THEIR SHADOW?

Bobbi

In 2018, we took our kids to Disneyland. We spent a lot of time on Radiator Springs Racers in Cars Land at California Adventure. The kids loved that ride... and my husband and I did too! The cars take a leisurely drive through Radiator Springs for the first half of the ride, then race against another car for the last half. We went on the ride several times during our trip and figured out that the car on the right always seemed to win.

It was our last ride; we were never going to ride again that trip. We were in the car, and I was so excited. We pull up to start the race, and we're on the left. I was like, "Crap. You know what that means. We're gonna lose." My five-year-old son leans over me, looks over at the other car and yells, "You're going down!" The cars start racing down the track, and the other car is in the lead for most of the ride. At the very last second, our car flies by the other one and we won! I was so excited, my son and I were screaming!

Strangely, all these lights started going off and the ride broke down and stopped at that moment. Maybe we made it malfunction by winning! They do such an amazing job on the rides at Disney, for a few moments we were truly first place racers!

BRAD

Have you ever taken a Disney vacation alone? I did! I was going to Orlando in 2009 for a conference, and I am a big Disney nerd, so I made sure I booked in an extra day to hit the Magic Kingdom. A friend of mine was a retired Disney employee and had a park-hopper pass that was good at the four major Walt Disney World parks, and he gave it to me for free! Now I had a decision to make: I had one day and four parks to choose from. Where should I go? The answer was obvious: All of them!

It was the final day of my trip, and I wanted to save money by not going back to my hotel for three measly hours before heading to the airport, so I took my suitcase with me. I started my day at the Animal Kingdom. I went to Guest Relations and they said they would hold my suitcase. I went in at park opening and headed for the Tree of Life, just to see the 300 animals carved into it. From there, I did the Kilimanjaro Safari and the Wildlife Express Train. They were both interesting enough, but there were more parks to see. I picked up my bag and went to the next stop.

I went to Disney Hollywood Studios next. After turning in my suitcase, I went straight to the Great Movie Ride. It was fantastic! Actual cast members took part in playing gangsters and heroes while taking us through real movie props. It was one of my favorite attractions, but sadly now it's gone. I also watched the Indiana Jones Epic Stunt Spectacular. I almost went on Star Tours, but the line was too long and there were more parks to see!

I wanted to ride a boat across the bay to get to Epcot, so I ended up going in the side entrance. Of course, I had to see Spaceship Earth. It was amazing how much they crammed into that attraction! It just keeps going up and up and up! I also rode Mission: SPACE (on the more exciting Orange team!) and then took a Viking voyage through Maelstrom. The line for Soarin' was way too long. Unfortunately, because I had come in the side entrance, I had to go back there to get my suitcase, then return to the main entrance so I could head to the final park of the day.

At Magic Kingdom, the first thing I remember was going under the train tracks, through Town Square, and coming onto Main Street to see... the wrong castle! From the wide view, everything was identical to the Disneyland I know and love, except the Cinderella's Castle at the end of the road is much bigger than Sleeping Beauty's. I understand why it's used for more promotional material. It's very impressive! I hit all the Disney mainstays: Pirates of the Caribbean, Haunted Mansion, and the Jungle Cruise. I just wanted to see what the differences were. And there were several! I realized that I hadn't eaten all day, so I practically inhaled a Mickey Mouse waffle and got ready to go to the airport.

It sounds terrible, but I loved going to Disney World by myself! I got to experience the parks exactly the way I wanted. No one pressured me to go on rides I didn't want to go on. No one complained that I was taking too long. I never had to wait outside a bathroom for someone who was taking forever! I am happy to go to the parks with my family because Disney is different depending on who you're with. But four Disney parks in one day by myself was a unique experience, and I'm glad I'll always have that magical memory!

WHO HAS LOST THEIR SHADOW?

CAROL

Disneyland has always been so special to me and always will be. When I was a kid, we went to Disneyland A LOT! We lived in Sacramento and would all load up in the station wagon and go. One year, my dad lost his job and there were four of us kiddos in the house, it was a tough time for sure. We thought Disneyland was not going to be a possibility for a long time. But I came home from school one day and my dad said, "I got a new job and we're going to Disneyland!"

We walked in and like ALWAYS, went straight to It's a Small World first for my mom. Back in the day they had a mule train ride, and that was my sister's favorite. So many amazing memories... One of the memories that is the most vivid in my mind is from December 15, 1966. It was the day that the Disney company changed forever. It was the day that Walt Disney died.

I was pretty young at the time, almost eight years old. I remember it being on the news and my mom crying when she told us that Walt had passed away. We were staying at the Disneyland Hotel and, as much as they tried to hide it, you could tell the cast members were upset. We all were. Inside Disneyland, all of the flags were lowered to half-mast in honor of their irreplaceable leader. It was all so sad. Even at that young age I could feel the heavy mood throughout the park. Disneyland pressed on, and so did the Disney Company. But that day, even the Happiest Place on Earth had a moment of sadness.

Carolyn

We were locked in Disneyland! Who hasn't dreamed about having the park to themselves? From 2000-2003, we were season passholders at Disneyland, making the 6 hour trek every other month. Our kids were little, and Disneyland was magic. It was our magical happy place until we moved farther away.

In 2005, we returned, thinking this might be the last family vacation. At forty-one, my husband had been diagnosed with prostate cancer, and given less than 20% chance of survival. We were determined to make the most out of this trip. The first day, we were there bright and early, first in line. A CM let us in by mistake, and we were the only guests inside for 5 minutes! (We had to stay right by the entrance, but it was still fun, and folks recognized us all day)

My husband's company has a membership at Club 33. We have been lucky to be able to access 33 a few times. This trip was an adventure. We had reservations at 7:30 and the park closed at 8. We had a nice leisurely dinner, complete with delicious chocolate martinis. By the time we left, it was close to 9:30, and we had to have an escort to leave the park.

We got to the gate, and it was locked with no security guard in site. Our escort went off to find security, and we were left to roam Main Street. Talk about a great photo op! The parade floats came by, repositioning for the next day. All in all, we were locked in for about 20 minutes. First ones in, last

ones out. If this was our last family trip, Walt certainly had sprinkled some memorable pixie dust!

Fast forward 10 years to the day, my husband and daughter ran the Star Wars half marathon, cancer free! Disney is still our magical happy place.

Celebrating their magical happy place

DISNEY WATER PARKS

River Country (closed) – 1976

Typhoon Lagoon – 1989

Blizzard Beach – 1995

DISNEY CRUISE SHIPS

Disney Magic – 1998

Disney Wonder – 1999

Disney Dream – 2011

Disney Fantasy – 2012

Clinton

I went to Disneyland when I was very young, probably about eight years old in 1975. I remember the rides, of course. The Tiki Room is still my favorite. I know it's not everyone's favorite, but I like it! What I remember most of all was this really disturbing evil queen from Snow White booth on Main Street. It was sort of like one of those fortune teller booths, but instead of a gypsy in a booth, it had the old hag version of the evil queen inside a cage. It was a miniature version of her, only about four feet tall, locked in the booth with chains on.

She would periodically come to life and try to convince you to let her out. She would beg and plead to be released in her crackly witch voice. There was a key in the lock that you could turn but she was safely locked inside. Her evil hag face just kept looking at you as she begged you to set her free.

That thing scared the bejeebers out of me!

I saw her there again the next time I went back in 1985, but now she is safely removed from the sights of young children. Thankfully she has permanently retired to my nightmares.

WHO HAS LOST THEIR SHADOW?

ⅅAVE

In 2012, I took my granddaughter to Epcot. She loved going on the rides and touring through the different countries of the World Showcase. We decided to have our meals in some of the various country pavilions. In the early afternoon, she wanted Chinese food for lunch from the China pavilion. That sounded tasty so we enjoyed a delicious Chinese lunch. Later that evening, when it was dinner time, I asked her what she wanted for dinner and she asked for Chinese food again. I wanted her to try some other foods (and I wanted to have something different) so I told her that she should not eat that much Chinese food in one day. She kindly informed me that Chinese people eat Chinese food all day every day!

Ethan

My parents own a timeshare in Orlando, so we are lucky to go to Disney World often. It has always been a highlight of my summer. We take turns deciding which park to visit. In 2010, it was my sister's turn to choose the park and she wanted to go to Magic Kingdom. There is only one thing I hate about Disney World... lines! I don't like standing in a line for an hour to ride something for two minutes. The FastPass is the most magical thing in the Magic Kingdom. If I do not have a FastPass, I don't want to ride.

Pirates of the Caribbean: At World's End was just coming out that year, and I was a typical six-year-old obsessed with pirates. As we were walking around Adventureland, we found a new attraction called The Pirate League. It was the coolest thing my six-year-old brain had ever seen! It was like the Bibbidi-Bobbidi-Boutique, but for boys. The first step in becoming a pirate was choosing a costume. I chose one where the bones glowed in the dark. After I looked like a pirate, they painted my entire face and gave me an official pirate name... Will Bladecutter! Once I was an official pirate, I got to take the pirate oath. It was awesome!

After going through the Pirate League, my dad thought it was a great idea to go on the Pirates of the Caribbean ride. I had never been on that ride before because back then FastPass was not an option. The wait time was sixty minutes, but being dressed like a pirate, I *had* to go. As soon as we got in line, a Disney cast member came up to me and said, "Jack Sparrow is

waiting for you." They took me and my family right to the front of the line, and we got into the boat ahead of everyone else! It was one of those days that just kept getting better. It was greater than having a FastPass... Jack Sparrow himself was waiting for me! For that one day at Disney World, I truly was a pirate.

Ethan the pirate

10 POPULAR PARK TREATS

Dole Whip

Churro

Mickey Mouse Pretzel

Popcorn

Mickey Mouse Ice Cream Bar

Caramel Apple

The Grey Stuff

Mickey Mouse Waffle

Turkey Leg

Mickey Mouse Rice Krispy Treat

Gini

In 1991, my husband and I drove our five-year-old daughter Annie from Pennsylvania to Orlando, Florida so we could spend a week at Walt Disney World. This was one those full family vacation weeks spent touring the Disney parks and seeing as many sights as we could see. We spent two days at Disney Kingdom, one at Epcot, one at MGM Studios, and one at Canyon River Rapids Water Park.

Annie got to see Mickey, and they even invited her to hold a banner and march for a few steps at the end of one of the parades. I loved taking her through some of the classic kiddie rides like It's a Small World and the Tea Cups. I thought for sure that would be what she liked best too.

I was not quite right about that.

When we got home, a good friend asked Annie what her favorite memory was of our trip. Annie said, "At the hotel, when you put a quarter in the bed, it shook!"

WHO HAS LOST THEIR SHADOW?

Jackie

My Favorite memory at Disneyland was in 1968. My husband was stationed in San Diego, and they had a San Diego Disney night. This was early December and our $19.95 ticket got me my first look at Disneyland in winter wonder.

I mostly remember Main Street, when we first entered the park. It was so beautiful. Twinkling lights lit up every tree. There was very little crowd and no parade that I recall. That was pretty far back, and it was only my second trip ever to Disneyland, so I was just so taken aback that something this simply beautiful sat in the middle of a busy world outside.

And did I mention we used very few of the tickets in the ticket book? This was back in the earlier days of the park when they were still using the ticket books to get on each ride. Our daughter was only three months old, and we had taken our fifteen-month-old nephew along, so we had no need for E tickets, the tickets for the more exciting rides.

To this day—fifty years later—I still have that book, and all of the E tickets are still in there!

PRESIDENTS OF
THE WALT DISNEY COMPANY

1923 – 1966: Walt Disney
1966 – 1971: Roy O. Disney
1971 – 1972: Donn Tatum
1972 – 1977: E. Cardon Walker
1977 – 1984: Ron W. Miller
1984 – 1994: Frank Wells
1994 – 1997: Michael Ovitz
1997 – 2000: Michael Eisner
2000 – 2012: Robert A. Iger

C.E.O.S OF
THE WALT DISNEY COMPANY

1929 – 1971: Roy O. Disney
1971 – 1976: Donn Tatum
1976 – 1983: E. Cardon Walker
1983 – 1984: Ron W. Miller
1984 – 2005: Michael Eisner
2005 – _____ : Robert A. Iger

Jaclyn

When I was in high school in 1996, we did grad night at Disneyland. Our last week of school as seniors, we had finals all week, and then on Thursday we had graduation.

We went to school in the morning for our last final, then we went home for a short break, went to school to have our graduation, went home to celebrate, and then had to be back at school at 9:30 that night. The bus left at ten. We got to Disneyland and waited with the other hordes of graduates for the gates to open at midnight.

We went in, but we'd had such an exhausting week that we took a break in the It's a Small World ride and fell asleep. They took us around a second time while we slept! We got off refreshed and enjoyed the rest of grad night until we met at the busses to go home at six in the morning.

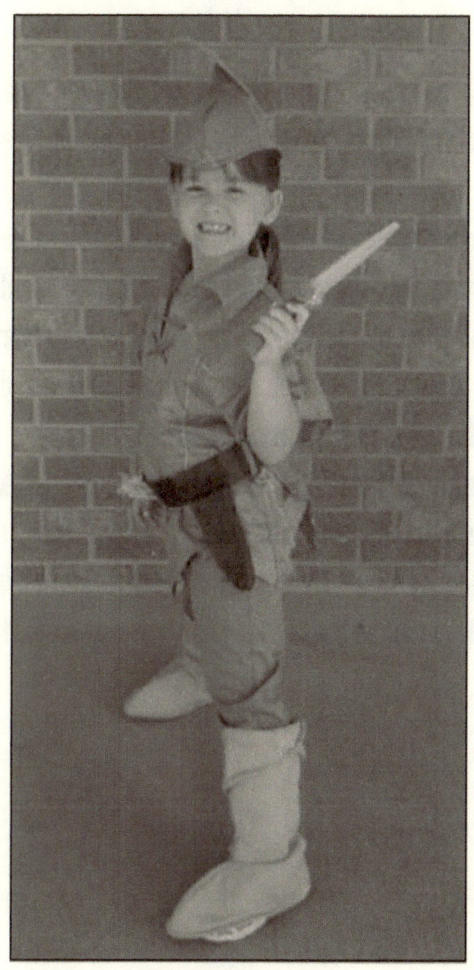

Lacey as Peter Pan

Jan

My daughter Lacey dressed up as Peter Pan for Mickey's Not-So-Scary Halloween Party in 2010 when she was seven. We walked through the park and enjoyed all of the costumes and the mountains of candy that were everywhere throughout the Magic Kingdom. My little Peter Pan and I were walking near Pirates of the Caribbean when, out of nowhere, Captain Hook appeared and challenged her to a duel. She had a tremendous time as a heroic swashbuckler, fighting against the vile Captain Hook. And, I'm proud to say, she won the duel against that codfish! I may have wiped away a few tears. She's almost sixteen now and remembers it well. Pure Disney magic!

WHO HAS LOST THEIR SHADOW?

♪ANELLE

Every year, my youth group would take a trip to southern California to do outreach work. We'd work in homeless shelters, retirement communities, and cleaning churches. The last day of the trip each year was spent going to Disneyland! I was very involved as a teenager, and I was obsessed with Disney, so I signed up every time the trip was offered!

So the year was maaaayybbeee 2013, and we were in line for the Tower of Terror at California Adventure. The line was long enough to be sending us back and forth through the courtyard, so pretty long. A few of us waited in line together with one of the trip sponsors because our youth pastor was too chicken to go on the ride! Everyone in line was doing what people do in lines. They talked, kept their kids from climbing on things, played games on their phones, and tried to keep cool in the California sun. So, when my hand got wet, I thought maybe I had been splashed by someone's water bottle, or they had a mister to keep cool.

Not even close.

I looked down and there was bird poop on my hand! A little bird had decided to poop on my hand in the middle of California Adventure! I couldn't believe it. After I realized what it was, I doused my hand in sanitizer. It was so gross, but I wasn't going to lose my spot in line. The ride was great and our sponsor screamed like a baby. But afterward I made sure to sterilize my hand!

Jason

Some of the most memorable moments at Disneyland happen when things don't go the way they're supposed to. I took my wife and daughters on Pirates of the Caribbean in 2018 and it was great. For a while.

We drifted through the Blue Bayou area, and saw the man on the porch. We got the warning from the skull and crossbones and went down the first drop into the caverns. We went down the second drop and rounded the bend where the skeleton crew mans the shipwreck in the storm. We came to the room where the pirate captain skeleton sits on his bed in his room full of treasure... and we stopped.

We sat there for what felt like about forty-five minutes, all the while "Yo ho, yo ho, a pirates life for me!" music kept blaring all around us. That's all that it was doing over and over. We were saying to each other, "Oh my gosh! This is crazy. How deep is the water? Could we get out?" We were seriously considering getting out of our boat when an announcement came on saying, "Whatever you do, stay in your boats!" We were like, "Shoot, they heard us!"

We weren't sure what we were going to do. The music was really starting to drive us insane. We looked around and didn't see an emergency exit, but knew there had to be one somewhere. Even if there was, we weren't supposed to get out of the boats, and we didn't know how we'd get to the land anyway.

The ride was so backed up that every boat was bumping the boats ahead and behind. It was a ridiculously long time before we got moving again, somewhere between thirty minutes and six years. Even once we got going, it was very slow. We found out later there had been a medical emergency in one of the other boats. They gave us three free FastPasses to make up for it, but we had been there so long, we didn't have time to use them!

Jazmin's Ear Collection

Jazmin

Back in 2014, when my husband and I were dating, he took me on a spontaneous road trip to Disneyland for our fourth date. I was so excited and nervous because we had just met two weeks prior at the Disney store in our hometown of Salt Lake City, Utah.

When we finally arrived at Disneyland, he asked me if I wanted anything, and I said, "Sure." I chose a pair of Minnie Mouse headband ears. I wore them throughout the whole trip and made a comment to him that I was going to wear them every time I came to Disneyland. He replied "Don't do that. I'll just buy you a new pair every time we come!"

I thought that was sweet of him to say, but I didn't think we'd ever go back to Disneyland again together. Well, he has kept that promise because we have gone to Disneyland countless times and on every trip he has bought me a new set of ears. I now have a huge Minnie Mouse ears collection! On July 4th, 2016, he took me to Disneyland and proposed to me at Snow White's wishing well... and of course, bought me another set of ears!

Jill, Pluto, and Kim

Jill

In 1993, my senior year in high school, my best friend Kim and I took first place in the Future Homemakers of America Alaskan state competition with a community service project. That earned us the right to attend the national convention in Anaheim that summer. Our home economics teacher was going to accompany us as a chaperone, but our school principal was still worried about supervision—even though we had both already graduated! Our principal insisted that if my friend and I were going to have our own hotel room, there must be an adjoining door between our room and our teacher's. We didn't care so much about this. We loved our teacher and were just excited to leave Alaska and go on an adventure.

When we got to our room in the Anaheim Hilton, they had given us a huge corner room, because that was the only one with an interior door that joined a single room. Our corner room had one entire wall of windows that faced Disneyland. It looked over the parking lot that is now California Adventure. And every night, if we left the curtains open, we could watch the Disneyland fireworks. We were very pleased that our school principal's concern had such a wonderful result. We felt like rock stars! Plus, we got our picture taken with Pluto.

Oh, and we won a national gold medal on our community service project too!

Joe

I hope the statute of limitations has worn off for this story, but in my defense, I was only eleven...

I grew up in southern California, so I had several opportunities to go to Disneyland as a kid. In 1975, I was at Disneyland with my two nephews. We were all the same age, about ten and eleven years old. Two of us were running around in the Hub area in front of the castle, where the Walt Disney Partners statue is now. At that time, it was a big empty space.

One of the Three Little Pigs was dancing around as they do, entertaining the kids. The suit that the Three Little Pigs wore was this big round thing, so they didn't have a lot of visibility in there. My nephew and I kept running up behind the pig and pulling his ear. He would quickly turn around to stop us and nearly topple over. We thought it was hilarious and we were laughing our heads off. We did it three times and just kept laughing. We could tell the pig was getting frustrated, but we just kept doing it.

All of the sudden, out of the blue comes Goofy to the pig's rescue. Goofy comes up, and he starts yelling at us in the Goofy voice: "Hey! What are you guys doing?" We looked right at him and intentionally pulled the pig's ear one more time.

Goofy puts his hand on my nephew's shoulder to stop him, so I grabbed Goofy's tooth and pulled his head up and down. Goofy pushed me, and I fell to the ground. My nephew yells at Goofy, "Hey, get your $#@%

hands off my uncle!" Goofy and the Three Little Pigs started coming at us, and we realized about that time that we were going to get in a lot of trouble, so we turned and ran to Frontierland. They started to come after us but didn't follow us very far.

We never got caught and that story has remained fairly secret for the last 40+ years. Until now...

WHO HAS LOST THEIR SHADOW?

Jonathan

My two buddies and I had always talked about back-packing through Europe. Our lifeguarding jobs were not going to fund that, so in 2015, we decided to backpack through Disney's Epcot theme park instead. The World Showcase at Epcot is set up to look like various countries from around the world. It seemed like a fun and affordable way to have a European adventure.

To make it a little more interesting we decided to pack a few extra T-shirts and have some fun on Instagram. We went from land to land taking pictures as though we were actually visiting the countries represented, especially the European countries. We took pictures in England, France, Italy, Belgium, Germany, etc. then posted the pictures on Instagram over ten days.

We totally had our friends convinced we were in Europe! Unless they are reading this story, most still believe we were there. Thanks to Disney for being so authentic!

Josh

We had made big plans to fly down to California and go to Disneyland in 2018. Our bags were packed, we were excited... and our five-year-old son, Forest, got sick. Not just like a small cough. He got SICK sick. He began pooping every thirty minutes or so, mixed with vomiting here and there. But it was too late to change our plans! So off we went. We took him to the restroom every thirty minutes throughout the flight to take care of his business. It was awful!

And it didn't stop.

When we finally got into the park, the frequency of the diarrhea had lightened up, but so had the available restrooms. Needless to say, we kept the Disneyland map handy to find the closest place for him to run to! We would be an hour into a line for a ride and hear Forest: "Mommy, I have to go!" My wife would quickly take him back through the line to the nearest restroom, he would take care of whichever emergency it was that time, then they would come back to find me. Over and over, all day long. Most of the time, the other people in line were understanding. We've all had experiences with sick kids.

Forest still had an amazing time. We went on Soarin' Over the World, and he was convinced that we had actually gone through the screen! We tried to take him on a second time and he was like, "We can't. We went through the screen. It's broken!" It took us a long time to convince him it was

just a movie! He just couldn't comprehend that we could go through the screen again and again.

Healthy or sick, it's really hard not to have a magical day at Disneyland!

Julia enjoying Disneyland with her family

Julia

My husband and I took our daughter, Dalisay, to Disneyland at the end of 2018. She was very little, not quite a year old, so we bought her a toy souvenir appropriate for an eleven-month-old girl... a bubble blowing wand shaped like Cinderella's carriage! It didn't take us too long to realize that the toy didn't work.

While in the park I asked one of the workers in a little booth, "Do you happen to know, if I go to City Hall and ask them to exchange it for a new one, will they do that?" I had already lost my receipt was afraid that I was out of luck.

The cast member asked what was wrong with the toy and I explained to him that it made a weird noise and didn't blow bubbles. Obviously broken! He looked at it for a moment and said, "You're right! This one is a bad one." He grabbed a new one off the shelf and handed it over to my baby girl. I took out money to pay for it, since I thought he was selling it to me again. (Disneyland can cost so much money, as a joke, my husband got a T-shirt to wear at the park that read, "Most expensive day ever!")

To my surprise he stopped me from paying for it again and told me, "Oh no, you already paid for it. You just got a bad one. You don't have to go to city hall anymore, I'm happy I could help." I was thrilled, not only that they replaced our broken toy, but that the Disneyland employee did so with politeness and a smile on his face!

WHO HAS LOST THEIR SHADOW?

Kati

My best memories of the Disney parks are all about my kids. We took them to Walt Disney World, and the park is so amazing to enjoy when experienced through the eyes of a child.

With my oldest, the first time she saw Cinderella's castle, her face just lit up. It's an icon for a reason. All of the joy and magic of Disney World is captured in that one enormous symbol.

My middle child was just three years old and already quite the ladies' man. He had all of the princesses kissing his face and leaving lipstick marks all over. He walked around showing them off like a badge of honor.

My youngest got to enjoy his very first roller coaster ride on Slinky Dog. He was not even the slightest bit nervous. When we asked if he was ready to go, he threw his hands in the air and yelled, "I'm so ready!"

Kaitlyn and her mom at Disneyland

Kaitlyn

I have gone to Disneyland several times with my family because we used to live in California. I still get grumbly remembering that on one of my first trips there, I was too short to go on Indiana Jones. This quite upset me. We were able to go back again on another trip, but that had its own flaws.

In 2010 (or sometime around then), I was about six years old. I don't know if I had a cold or some sort of throw-up disease, but I was pretty miserable that day. My parents didn't want to get wet and get sicker, so while my mom and brother went on Splash Mountain, my dad took me to Winnie the Pooh. As a sicko seven-year-old, I was happy to sit and watch Pooh and there was no line, so after it was done my dad took me again... and again. By the time the rest of my family got off of Splash Mountain, we had gone through Pooh six times in a row!

We went to visit Mickey Mouse later, and I can't remember that part as well, but I mostly remember Mickey bending down to hug me but instead of hugging him, I honked his nose! My parents were all like, "KAITLYN! Don't do that!" I blame being too sick and delirious to think clearly!

The last thing I remember from that day was Tarzan's Treehouse.... We were climbing along in the treehouse and my stomach decided "Hm... This would be a great place to explode!" Then I threw up...in Tarzan's Treehouse.

It was a hard day overall, but when you're at Disneyland, none of that matters!

Katya

My favorite Disney Memory is from the first time I visited Magic Kingdom as a Cast Member!

It was May 2011, orientation day, the first day of our Disney College Program. We started our day at the Disney University in Orlando where the Mouse himself came to visit us. Our new boss, Mickey Mouse, came to our introduction class to welcome us to the Disney Team! We learned about the program, played games, and introduced ourselves. After class we received a tour of the Magic Kingdom, the park we would be working at. That's when the real magic happened.

I was twenty-two years old, far from a child, and this was not my first time at Disney. However, this time, walking into the park through the backstage entrance, it felt like the first time.

This was unlike anything I've ever experienced. Everything I once knew was now ten times better and brighter... The bright colors of the buildings on Main Street, the millions of bubbles in the air, the bundles of balloons all throughout the park, the music and dancing that spreads through the lands, the delicious smell of popcorn and cotton candy, and of course the Castle! Cinderella's beautiful Castle sits in the center of Magic Kingdom, uniting all of the lands. The way it sparkles and changes colors is the most magnificent spectacle in the park. I remember walking towards it,

sparkles glistening in my eyes, my mouth in a huge grin. I was like a little child in a candy store on her birthday.

My friend Brianna was in the group tour with me, and we were both so mesmerized that this beautiful, magical land was going to be our home for the next year that we couldn't resist. We stopped on the bridge next to the Castle and each took a picture of us in front of it.

I will never forget that day. Working for Mickey Mouse in the most magical place on earth was a dream come true. Getting an opportunity to work in my favorite park at Disney, surrounded by song and dance, and so much magic was an absolute fairytale! As Walt Disney once said, "If you can dream it, you can achieve it!"

Ashley's princess pic

Kim

As Disney regulars, we are always excited when Disney launches something new. In 2007, when my daughter Ashley was four years old, Disney launched the "Bibbidi Bobbidi Boutique" at the Magic Kingdom in Walt Disney World. We really didn't know what to expect when we made the reservation, but we were up for an adventure. Ashley came dressed as Aurora from *Sleeping Beauty* and was ready to be transformed into a fairytale princess.

As soon as we walked in, Ashley's fairy godmother welcomed her inside an enchanted beauty salon full of princesses and their fairy godmothers. Once situated in the magical chair, the pampering began. She was given a new hairstyle, nail color, accessories, and a tiny splash of make-up. Conversations with her stylists ranged from Prince Phillip to Snow White to Cinderella. Ashley asked her most curious princess questions, which were met with highly entertaining answers.

While the makeover was happening, Ashley was turned away from the mirror. Once the final reveal was ready, Ashley's fairy godmother sprinkled her with magical glitter, tapped her with a wand, and spun her around to the mirror. All you heard was a high pitch gasp. Disney had done it again! They had made my little girl's dreams come true.

Kristyn and her friend with Aladdin and Jasmine

Kristyn

On my eighteenth birthday, in 2008, I went with a friend to the Magic Kingdom. We ran around the park and did all the rides we could manage. The whole time, I watched the clock to make sure I knew the exact minute of my birth. I officially turned eighteen while waiting on line to meet Aladdin and Jasmine. At that moment, I said to my best friend, "I'm officially eighteen now!"

The cast member overseeing the line asked my name, and I gave it to her. She announced to this massive line that it was my birthday and asked everyone to join in singing to me. The entire line broke out singing Happy Birthday to me! It was amazing, and when I got to the front, Aladdin told me he had a gift for me but that Abu ran off with it.

WHO HAS LOST THEIR SHADOW?

Kristi

Eighteen-year-olds don't always make the best decisions.

In 1994, I had just got out of high school, and the graduates from our church youth group went on a trip from Washington state to Disneyland. Several of us were wandering around the park together and thought it might be fun to do the Davy Crockett Explorer Canoes. We piled in and started canoeing our way around the Rivers of America.

Somewhere near Tom Sawyer's Island, one of my friends dared me to jump overboard into the water. What was I supposed to do? I had been dared! I jumped overboard and landed in the cool water. Soaking wet, I immediately climbed back in the boat, laughing uncontrollably. The cast member controlling the boat was so mad. He yelled at me for disobeying the park rules, but fortunately did not kick me out of the park. I was soaking wet for hours after that!

It's definitely not something I would do today. And it's something I would yell at my own eighteen-year-old for doing now. But, caught up in the moment, I had to take the dare!

DISNEY PARK ATTRACTIONS
THAT LATER BECAME MOVIES

Mr. Toad's Wild Ride
1996

Tower of Terror
1997

Mission to Mars
2000

The Country Bears
2002

Pirates of the Caribbean
(The Curse of the Black Pearl)
2003

The Haunted Mansion
2003

Pirates of the Caribbean
(Dead Man's Chest)
2006

Pirates of the Caribbean
(At World's End)
2007

Pirates of the Caribbean
(On Stranger Tides)
2011

Tomorrowland
2015

Pirates of the Caribbean
(Dead Men Tell No Tales)
2017

Lénika

Disney can be fun, but it can also be draining. All day long in the hot sun, running around, eating junk food... In 2015, my boyfriend and I spent an entire day in Walt Disney World at Magic Kingdom Park, and we absolutely loved it! We rode rides and saw shows that you can't experience anywhere else. But it wore us out!

On the monorail, at the end of the day, we were so exhausted! We walked onto the full train like zombies and managed to find two empty seats. We sat down, but an older couple walked in looking even more worn out than us. My boyfriend stood up so the lady could sit.

She sat next to me and talked with us as the monorail took us away from the park. She asked me where we were from (we're from Mexico) and asked me how our vacation had been in Orlando. She was genuinely interested to know things about me. She was so grateful, she showed me her lanyard and asked me to choose a pin from it. I told her, "No, no, you really don't have to give me anything." But she insisted, so I told her if she really wanted to give me one, she should choose the pin that I would get. She said, "Okay, well I choose Cinderella because she's a princess and princesses are kind like you are."

That pin brings so much more happiness than any other souvenir I've bought at the park. It reminds me not only of a wonderful place, but of a wonderful person. A Disney fan like myself. Disney people are so amazing!

Linda's family vacation

LINDA

My favorite memory from a Disney park is watching my husband become himself again. My husband was involved in a terrible accident. He fractured his back, had shoulder decompression surgery, and two knee surgeries. He was retired out from a career he loved, unable to do FIRE/EMS any longer. He was also not allowed to ride his motorcycle.

Our youngest son and family decided a family Disney World vacation was warranted. Our entire family—children, spouses and grandchildren—was invited along to spend a few days at the Happiest Place on Earth. During that trip we watched the true recovery begin with my husband. While the primary reason was family, it was also the magical place. My husband even said, "Walt was right. Pass through these gates and forget your worries and troubles".

It began a family tradition of Disney vacations AND a tradition of us going solo at least once a year. We are counting down the days until our thirty-fifth wedding anniversary in September when we will celebrate it with Mickey's Not-So-Scary Halloween Party and dinner at Be Our Guest. I see people complain about crowds, lines, and everything else, BUT I was always be thankful to Disney for helping our family recover!

WHO HAS LOST THEIR SHADOW?

Lora

Once I became a grandmother, I could not wait to take my two grandsons to Disney World. We patiently waited until 2003 when the two boys were ages four and three. The first park we went to was Disney's Animal Kingdom. We were there right at opening and followed the crowd to the safari ride. It was perfect. The animals were all eating breakfast, and the park was beautiful.

When the ride was over, we headed to the Dinoland part of the park. My oldest grandson saw that they could dig for dinosaur bones and both boys immediately wanted to dig. They were so excited about digging that we were there for more than two hours! I was sitting there watching them, thinking about how much money I had just spent for the boys to play in a sandbox!

We continued to see other parks that week, but when we asked them about the experience, their overall trip highlight was digging for dinosaur bones!

Luke and his sister in the front of the monorail

Luke

We had spent two great days at Disneyland in 2015. I was thirteen and had been to Disneyland several times before, but had never ridden on the monorail. We had tried to get on it the first day, but it was closed before we left the park. We wanted to ride it from the Disneyland Hotel into the park that morning but staying at the hotel gave us special early entry into the park before the monorail was running.

My dad had heard that if you ask the platform attendant, you can ride in the front with the driver so, of course, we had to try to do that. We went up to the platform and discovered there was already a group waiting to be in the first car. The cast member working on the platform told us there was only going to be one more train that night but we could be in the front if we wanted to wait. We waited!

When the last train of the night showed up, the front car opened, and the cast member let us on board. As we were getting on, a small boy from a family behind us wanted to come in too but the platform attendant told them only one family was allowed to ride there. The little boy cried and cried as his family took him to the second Monorail car.

We only rode in the front of the monorail to the Downtown Disney stop, and the driver didn't say a word to us, but it was fantastic! It was the perfect way to end the trip!

MOVIES THAT BECAME RIDES

Snow White and the Seven Dwarfs
The Adventures of Ichabod and Mr. Toad
Alice in Wonderland
Peter Pan
Dumbo
Pinocchio
Star Wars
Song of the South
Who Framed Roger Rabbit
Raiders of the Lost Ark
Toy Story
Dinosaur
The Many Adventures of Winnie the Pooh
Armageddon
Finding Nemo
Monsters Inc.
The Little Mermaid
Ratatouille
Frozen
Cars
Tron
Avatar
The Three Caballeros
Guardians of the Galaxy
The Incredibles
Ant-Man and the Wasp
Inside Out

MADDISON (AGE 5)

I waited in line for the Ariel ride with my aunt. There were fish and Ursula.

TV SHOWS THAT BECAME RIDES

The Twilight Zone
Chip 'n Dale: Rescue Rangers

Melissa

My husband, Andrew, and I met in college. Very early on, we fell in love with the magic and atmosphere of all things Disney. We honeymooned to Disney World and have been blessed with the ability to make it to a Disney park at least once a year since we've been married—sometimes even more! But perhaps the most magical moment for me in a Disney park was the very first trip we got to take together.

Before Andrew and I had met, I had been planning a trip down to Disneyland with some of my friends. In between that summer of planning and our trip, Andrew and I had started dating. About two months before our 2011 spring break vacation, one of our friends couldn't make it, so Andrew jumped in and took her spot. It had been years since I got to visit Disneyland, and it was even more special having him there with me.

On one of our last nights there, Andrew and I found a spot on Main Street to watch the fireworks. I had bought a caramel apple before we sat down, but I can't just bite into them, I have to eat them cut up. So, I was sitting on the curb trying to cut my apple with a plastic butter knife. (Andrew, to this day, still makes fun of me for it—but hey, it worked! And I thoroughly enjoyed that caramel apple!) Anyways, we continued sitting on the curb watching all the people around us, getting excited for the evening festivities. Cast Members were selling all sorts of light up gadgets, and I made some dumb comment about how I didn't think they were ever worth

the money they cost since you only use them for one night...but in my head I always secretly wanted one anyways.

A few minutes later, Andrew got up to go to the restroom, and I held down the fort. When he returned, he came with a light up rose. He told me he was planning to buy it for me even before I made my comment, but that he wanted me to have something to remember the moment he told me he loved me for the very first time. He told me I didn't need to say anything back, just that he wanted me to know. My heart melted. He was my first boyfriend, my first love, and I was smitten. Within a few minutes we then stood and watched the fireworks burst over Sleeping Beauty's castle. It was the most magical moment for me EVER! To this day, I still have the fake light up rose sitting in a vase in our living room, and I plan to always keep it.

Melissa and Andrew with the light-up rose

WHO HAS LOST THEIR SHADOW?

Michelle

My Disney memory is not so much about Disneyland, but about what happened after.

I went to Disneyland with my sister, brother in law, dad, and uncle. We didn't want to waste a minute, so we arrived when the doors opened, had a blast, and stayed until the park closed. We must have had too great of a day because by the time we walked back out to the parking lot, not one of us could remember what our rental car looked like, including make, model, and color!

We also forgot where we parked.

These were the days before the giant parking garage when the parking lots circled the whole park. We didn't know if we parked in the Goofy, Donald, or Chip and Dale section. We wandered around from parking lot to parking lot at midnight using the key chain button until our rental car finally lit up and beeped.

Lesson learned... no matter how excited you are to meet Mickey, take the time to pay attention to the important details!

ATTRACTIONS CREATED FOR THE 1964-65 WORLD'S FAIR

It's A Small World
sponsored by Pepsi-Cola

Great Moments with Mr. Lincoln
sponsored by the state of Illinois

Progressland
sponsored by G.E.
(later became the Carousel of Progress)

Magic Skyway
sponsored by Ford
(partially became the prehistoric world
diorama along the Disneyland railway)

Mindy

I was on a trip with my church youth group when I was fourteen. I didn't understand the concept of sunscreen on a cloudy day, so when we went to the beach and it was overcast, it didn't even hit my preteen brain a burn was a possibility. I'm very pale, so the sun really burns when it wants. I spent the beach day in the sun and when I woke up in the morning, my face had blisters, I was crispy and my eyes were literally sealed shut. I had never had that bad of a burn. I don't know if anyone in the history of youth trips had had that bad of a sunburn.

But everyone else was going to Disneyland, and I was not going to stay behind! So I went with them, but the minute I passed through the gate, I felt like throwing up, so they took me to the infirmary. I spent the day in the infirmary in Disneyland with what the Disneyland nurse labeled "sun poisoning." I paid $30 (it was 1990!) to spend the whole day in the Disney nurse's office, and it wasn't even a Disney style office. They didn't even have Mickey Band-Aids!

Gratefully, at the end of the day, in the last few hours, my friends came to rescue me. One of the sponsors "broke me out," and then they did a speed tour of Disneyland. We ran from land to land, making sure we went through every one. I didn't get to ride a whole lot, but I at least felt like I had fun at the park, and it was a nice finish. Needless to say—I'm a fan of sunscreen now.

WHO HAS LOST THEIR SHADOW?

Nicole L.

My daughter is a HUGE Pooh fan. In 2010 she was turning five years old, and we took her on her first trip to Walt Disney World to celebrate the big day! We scrimped and saved in order to make the trip possible. As an extra little bonus, we also surprised her with a new stuffed Pooh Bear and took her to ride The Many Adventures of Winnie the Pooh. I spent the ride completely ignoring the heffalumps and woozles. Instead I was watching my daughter's face as she went through the entire ride in happy tears. Her face, the magic in her eyes... it was worth every single penny we had saved.

WORLD SHOWCASE AT EPCOT

World Showcase
contains 11 pavilions:

Canada
China
France
Germany
Italy
Japan
Mexico
United States
United Kingdom
(all built in 1982)
Morocco (added in 1984)
Norway (added in 1988)

E.P.C.O.T. was originally conceived
by Walt Disney as a working city called:

Environmental Prototype
Community Of Tomorrow

Nicole P.

We went to Walt Disney World in 2006 and had an interesting experience. We stayed at the Caribbean Beach Resort, but the hotel was so full that the only room available for us was a room with two full-sized beds. There was no other option, it was totally booked up. My two daughters had to share a full-sized bed, and my husband and I had to share a full-sized bed. For five days we were crammed together in that... family bonding experience. We still managed to make the best of it because we were really there for the parks.

My daughter, Sophie, was about seven years old and very excited to be at Disney World. She was running, as kids do, when she fell on the sidewalk and cracked her head open, so she had a huge red bump the rest of the day. Every character all day long would come over to her because she had this giant huge nasty goose egg. They were so kind and sweet to our daughter. She was the cute little girl with curly hair so they would pick her up and hold her and hug her. It gave her a lot of extra attention!

WHO HAS LOST THEIR SHADOW?

Pamela

I went to Disney's Animal Kingdom with my family in 2004. We decided to go on the Kilimanjaro Safari so we could see some of the cool animals they have on display. I don't think this ride does this anymore, but the Kilimanjaro Safari used to have a part of the ride where the truck would go over a rickety bridge. It would rock side to side and seem like the bridge was about to break. The driver would tell you to "lean to the right!" My mom forgot about this part of the ride and when it happened, she totally freaked out. She grabbed me so hard and yelled so loud that I could not stop laughing.

Rachael

My dad had a video tape of me in Disney World when I was six months old. I fell in love with the Main street electrical parade. Every time I heard that music I would burst into tears of wishing and hoping to one day see that parade.

At the age of seventeen, I was finally able to get back to Disney World. As amazing and magical as it was, it sadly was missing the parade since it moved to Disneyland in California.

Fast forward to 2009, my sister and I hit the road for a month-long cross-country road trip. During this trip we wanted to make it to Disneyland, but I discovered that, shockingly, the electrical parade was now back in Florida. At this point I didn't care; I just couldn't wait to visit Walt's park! And so, we spent two days in the Happiest Place on Earth. On our last day, my sister and I settled into our spot for the night fireworks. Julie Andrews' voice came over the loudspeakers to introduce the fireworks and then we got to hear Walt Disney himself during his opening speech. As I listened to his words, all I could think was how wonderful it was to be standing in his park, hearing his voice.

The fireworks started and we heard opening sounds to each attraction throughout the park. All of a sudden the castle went black, and as it lit up in every color Crayola could think of, the music from the Main street electrical parade came on. My sister looks over at me, and I burst into tears.

She instantly grabbed onto me and held me. No amount of words can express the overwhelming joy I had at that moment. It wasn't exactly my childhood dream, but it was better than I could have ever imagined it. Several years later, when I think of that moment, I still tear up a little. Disney will always be in my heart and my memories.

WHO HAS LOST THEIR SHADOW?

Samantha

We went to Disney's Hollywood Studios in 2018 and had our two-year-old little boy with us. We went to get a picture by the ship in front of the 50s Prime Time Cafe before we went in to eat. The cast member taking the picture noticed that my son wasn't wearing any shoes and asked what had happened to them. I told her that he had lost them earlier that day. The photographer asked where we planned to go after the picture, and I told her we were going to eat at the diner. Well, it was maybe ten mins later when she found us in the Prime Time Café, waiting for our table. She handed me a pair of Mickey Mouse Crocs for our son. She was so sweet, and I never got her name to let her boss know the amazing thing she did. I will always remember how she made our day just a little more magical!

Sara

For my birthday in 2012, I really wanted to eat at Blue Bayou. It was one of the only things I had never done at Disneyland. I'm from Anaheim, had an annual pass when they were laminated cards with Polaroid pictures, and even worked at the park for a bit, so I wanted to complete my "done it all" mantra.

My boyfriend and I dressed up, went to the park, and headed full steam to Blue Bayou. When we neared the restaurant, my boyfriend started to video tape me, and said, "Ring the Club 33 doorbell!" This was when the Club 33 door was next to Blue Bayou.

I'm like, "No way!" because I don't want this to be a spoof or game where we film Sara making a fool of herself ringing the Club 33 doorbell. Yet, he kept asking me to do it. I was so adamant that I will not ring it, he did it instead. He gave our party name into the speaker, and when the door opened, I was like, "Holy $#@%!!!" It turned out my boyfriend was able to work a connection through one of his co-workers. When they let us in, I was squealing for joy and jumping up and down. It was ridiculously cute. He videotaped me holding the Club 33 menu and saying, "We're actually here!" It was awesome!

Fast forward to the end of the night, and my boyfriend started to show me a magic trick he'd been working on. Throughout his trick, I was trying not to roll my eyes and blurt out, "Really? You're doing this during

dinner at Club 33?" He took out a deck of cards and had me choose one (it was the three of diamonds). He then tried to guess my card by pulling the two of diamonds out of the deck. Oh no, where was my card? He told me to look for the missing one. He had given me a jewelry box earlier that day for my birthday, and I honestly thought I'd find a small playing card inside. Little did I know he was actually proposing! When I opened the box, I found a beautiful engagement ring inside. He got down on his knee and asked me to marry him. Of course I said yes! It was really interesting to have the attention of the entire room of the most elite club in Disneyland because your soon-to-be husband loves you. They truly pampered us the rest of the evening, and we had a wonderful time.

And I still haven't been to the Blue Bayou!

Sara's birthday treat

Scott's mug collection

Scott

I have been to Disney World with my children a few times. We like to rent a condo in Orlando and take several days to enjoy the parks. Typically, my favorite part is after the noise and crowds of the park when I can sit in the quiet Jacuzzi with a beer at the end of the day.

During one particular trip in 2011, our travel plans just coincidentally coincided with the International Beer and Wine Festival at Disney's Epcot theme park. My dad and I broke away from our family and went around sampling beers from around the world. Each beer came in a souvenir plastic beer mug with the country's flag on the side. We kept stuffing the mugs in my backpack after each beer.

Not only was this my favorite Disney day ever, but these mugs quickly became my favorite beer mug collection!

Seatta's granddaughter with Tigger

SEATTA

In 2006 we took our two-year-old granddaughter and eighteen-month-old grandson to Disney World for the first time. This was brave of us because they were both in diapers and religiously took naps at one p.m. each day. Since they were both under three years old, they did not need a Disney park ticket for entry. Our plan was to take the kids to the park in the morning, then return the kids back to their mom and dad for lunch and go back ourselves for the rest of the day. My main goal was to get some cute pictures of the kids with the Disney characters.

We found a place that had three Winnie the Pooh characters in a row. Perfect! Not perfect... All I wanted was a cute picture to remember our first trip to Disney. But the kids did not like the "scary" costumed characters. Accepting defeat, we turned to leave. Just as we were headed for the exit, Tigger all of a sudden went behind my granddaughter and pulled up her ponytails. I quickly snapped the picture! My granddaughter was not as excited as I was. All I heard was her sweet voice say, "Oh, Tigger, look what you did to my hair!"

WHO HAS LOST THEIR SHADOW?

SHARA

It's not often you get to say, "I was there!" for the opening of a Disney park, but when it comes to Disney's California Adventure, I can proudly say "I was there!" ...and that might be the most exciting part about that day.

There isn't much to tell about that day honestly. It was February 8, 2001, and my boyfriend (at the time) and I went to see the new park. I was an annual passholder back then too. We expected a huge crowd of people to be waiting at the entrance so we got there early, way before opening.

But there was no crowd! There was hardly anyone there!

The park was pretty empty all day, so we took our time and saw every attraction there was to see, including Superstar Limo, of course! I actually thought it was funny in a lame sort of way. We saw the giant bronze sun in the entry way, the Golden Gate Bridge for the monorail, and the huge CALIFORNIA letters out front. We went on Soarin' Over California the Orange Stinger. We saw all the shows, including Golden Dreams with Whoopi Goldberg, which I thought was a pretty neat story. California Screamin' was the smoothest roller coaster I'd ever ridden! Being one of the first to ride it meant it wasn't all worn down and used. It was like skating on polished ice.

While I wasn't overly impressed by DCA that day, it was pretty neat to see something so different from Disneyland and experience something completely new.

Socks

In 2018, I spent a Sunday afternoon at Disneyland celebrating the nine-year anniversary of my first date with Molly. It is hard to believe that it was nine years previous on June 24, 2009 when I met Molly in person for the very first time in front of Sleeping Beauty's Castle.

We had been matched by eHarmony during the last week of April, and I first communicated with her through the eHarmony website on May seventeenth. Five weeks later, after 150 pages of emails and numerous phone calls, we finally met in person at the castle on that sunny summer morning.

Although it may seem unusual to most people to spend an entire day together for a first date, it seemed perfectly natural to us. We had shared so much of ourselves with each other during the previous five weeks, had so much in common in virtually every area of our lives, including a shared love of Disneyland. We appeared to be very compatible on every level, so we figured that, even if there was no chemistry between us when we finally met, we would still become very close friends.

As it turned out, we had a lot of chemistry! After spending about fifteen minutes walking through the Park holding hands with Molly, I was convinced that she would become my wife.

Exactly six months later, on the morning of December 24, 2009, Molly and I returned to Sleeping Beauty's Castle to have pictures taken to commemorate the sixth month anniversary of our first date... At least that's

what I told Molly. Instead, I proposed to Molly in the exact same spot where we first met and had a Disneyland photographer lined up in advance to record the event.

One year later, on December 24th, 2010, Molly and I were married in Burbank, CA in a private, intimate ceremony, with only our immediate family present. As you can probably imagine, I have a lot of memories of the times that I spent with Molly at Disneyland over the years... All of them good!

Socks and Molly get engaged

WHO HAS LOST THEIR SHADOW?

Sorsha

In 2015, I was ten and had the chance to perform at Disneyland with my fifth grade choir. The whole choir got to go to the park and sing, and then when we were done, we were able to go on rides. It was so cool!

After the performance, I saw a girl that I had not seen in about five years. She didn't see me, so I separated from my group and followed her. We were not supposed to separate from the group, and eventually I lost my group entirely. I would have gone back to the group, but the girl recognized me, so we stood there talking for a few minutes in front of Sleeping Beauty's castle.

One of the choir leaders came to find me, and he was mad! He started yelling at me in front of my friend and half of Disneyland! I was so embarrassed!

STEVEN

It was a long and unusually hot day in the Magic Kingdom. It was the first day of March, and we'd expected it to be warm, seeing that it was Orlando, but it was a little hotter than normal. At the end of the day with our four-month-old son in tow, my wife, Jordan, wanted to ride Splash Mountain. We had a FastPass, and her parents were with us so we could ride it together while they watched our son. However, I wasn't feeling so great and told her that she should just go by herself. I thought she'd enjoy it more.

"Fine," she said.

When your wife tells you "Fine." with the simple period at the end, you know you're in trouble. We were in Adventureland, sitting near the Enchanted Tiki Room, and she took off towards Frontierland and Splash Mountain. I started to push the stroller over to the queue at Splash Mountain to wait for her, knowing when she got off I was going to get SOMETHING. Mostly a stern talking to, I thought. But when she came off the ride and walked up to me with a smirk, I knew something was up.

She held up her phone and showed me the picture and said, "Here! I did this for YOU!" She had made the angriest face in her Splash Mountain photo. We both burst out laughing!

We made our way to the train and out of the park. Back in our room, I put the photo online, thinking some friends and family would get a kick out of it. By the time we got to the airport the next day to fly home, the picture

had started to go viral, and Jordan became the internet meme known as "Angry Splash Mountain Lady."

The infamous "Angry Splash Mountain Lady" pic

Tiffany

In November 2015 we lost our third child shortly after he was born. So in November 2016 on our baby's first birthday and "angelversary" we decided to surprise our older children with a trip to Disneyland, because we all felt that we needed to do something just for fun.

We didn't tell the kids until, like, a day or two before we left—they were wondering why we were packing. When we got to Disneyland, my kids were super excited, as were my husband and I. We going to the park! The first place we went when we got in was a line to see Minnie Mouse and then Mickey Mouse. My son loved seeing Mickey and Goofy, and both kids enjoyed the Dumbo and Carousel rides.

What makes this memory special to me is that it was our first family trip together and we were celebrating our baby's first birthday and angelversary. None of us felt sad or scared. We were happy! We laughed and we talked about our baby, Madison Connor, wishing him a happy birthday. My husband even got First Visit and Birthday buttons for him.

Since it was the first week of November, most of our favorite rides were unavailable due to the park being decorated for Christmas. I remember when we first walked in, looking down Main Street at the beautiful castle and the big Christmas tree in the center, and just thinking of how magical it all looked. Given what we had been through the past year, it was a happy sight for us to enjoy together. We focused on the good and not the sad, and we

were able to enjoy the rides, our two oldest, and share with them our memories and experiences with Disney from when we were little. Before we left, we got each of our kids mouse ears with their names on them.

Mouse ears for Tiffany's children

WHO HAS LOST THEIR SHADOW?

Tina

In the summer of 2017, I was with my sister's family at Walt Disney World. My niece, who was six, didn't quite understand how wait times worked. We walked by Olaf, and she noted the thirty-minute wait. We were on our way to lunch at 50s Prime Time, so we couldn't go just then. Later in the day, she said "Thirty minutes must be up, we can go see Olaf now!"

We went back to swim in the pool and later that night, I took my niece to Disney Hollywood Studios for some fun. She still wanted to see Olaf, so we got in line. I told the Cast Member what my niece had said about the wait time, and the Cast Member asked us to wait there for a minute. She came back, and let us into the FastPass line, telling my niece that she was the special princess that Olaf had been waiting for that day. They even came by and asked for her autograph! It makes me cry even to this day!

Tom playing with his grandson

Tom

We went with my daughter's family to Walt Disney World in 2006. One of her kids was almost three, and the other was just one and a half, but he was still able to get into mischief. In the Magic Kingdom park there was a Winnie-the-Pooh play area like you would find at park. My daughter asked me to watch my grandson while she took my granddaughter to the bathroom. We played together and had fun on the slide. A few minutes later I noticed that my daughter returned to the play area and assumed that her return meant she was back watching my grandson.

I should not have assumed that without asking her directly.

About five minutes later my daughter asked, "Where is Ethan?" and I replied, "I thought you were watching him since you were back from the bathroom."

Sheer panic!

My wife and daughter started to scurry around the playground, calling for Ethan. Out of the corner of my eye, I saw a Disney cast member on a walkie-talkie, then two other cast members with a little boy. Ethan had wandered out of the Winnie-the-Pooh playground and into the main walkway of Fantasy land. We rushed right over to the Disney cast members, and they were absolutely phenomenal. The safety and security team at Disney is top notch!

WHO HAS LOST THEIR SHADOW?

Vicki

In 1996, my seven-year-old son Jake entered a contest in *Family Fun* magazine. He had to write a story about which Winnie the Pooh character his best friend reminded him of. The winner received a trip to Disney World for him and his best friend. Jake wrote about his best friend Kyle, who was in the hospital with pneumonia. He said Kyle reminded him of Eeyore because the last time he saw him, he seemed sad! They chose one person from every state, and Jake was the Oregon winner. Each winner could bring their bestie, so there were 100 kids invited to the park as contest winners.

The trip was a promotion for the upcoming Winnie the Pooh movie, *Pooh's Grand Adventure: The Search for Christopher Robin*. As part of the trip, everyone got to see the movie before it came out in theaters. Jake was only seven, so the part he remembers best from that trip is watching the movie and being super scared to ride the Tower of Terror!

We stayed at a Disney hotel and were treated as VIP's for four days. Kathie Lee Gifford and her kids, Cody and Cassidy, put on a private concert for us at Epcot. We were ushered to the front of the lines, put in VIP viewing for firework shows and parades, and went to the water park. Every meal was an extravaganza of fancy kid food and Disney characters!

PLANNED DISNEY PARKS
WHICH NEVER GOT BUILT

Mineral King Ski Resort
Sequoia National Park, CA

Riverfront Square
St. Louis, MO

Disney's America
Haymarket, VA

Westcot
Anaheim, CA

Port Disney
Long Beach, CA

Disney-MGM Studio Tour
Burbank, CA

Disney's Arabia
Dubai, UAE

Disneyland Singapore
Singapore

Victoria

In 1967, when I was seven years old, my family joined our cousins for a trip to Disneyland. We arrived at the front gate and split into four groups to go through the park. We began walking down Main Street, looking at all of the shops. When we came to the candy store, I rushed in and exclaimed to my mother, "Look at all the colors!"

But she wasn't behind me. She hadn't seen me go in.

I ran out, trying to find my family, but they were gone, and no one realized I was missing. Everyone had just assumed I was in a different group. A Disney Cast member paged my family, but I didn't know my parents' names, so they could only state my first name.

I was assigned a young, freckle-faced, red-headed, teenage boy to keep me company. I would cry and laugh and cry again. And throughout it all, he stayed with me. He took me on rides and brought me food and snacks and drinks all day trying to keep me happy.

No one in my family realized I was missing until they met up at Mark Twain's riverboat... at 10:00 p.m.!

I would love to find that young man, if he's still alive, and tell him, "Thank you, thank you, thank you! For your kindness, your patience, and your caring. I've never forgotten you!"

Brad Libs

Use the answers below to fill in the blanks on the next page
and add your own story to the book!

Number _____

Disney Park _____

Someone you know _____

Disney ride _____

Number _____

Noun _____

Disney character _____

Number _____

Disney park food _____

Adjective _____

Number _____

Disney ride _____

Exclamation _____

Number _____

Disney character _____

Adjective _____

MY DAY AT DISNEY

When I was _____. years old, I went to
(number)

_____ with my friend _____. It was so much fun!
(Disney park)   (someone you know)

We rode on _____ almost _____ times before I got
(Disney ride)   (number)

sick and threw up a _____. I got to meet _____ and
(noun)   (Disney character)

_____ with my favorite character, _____!
(verb)   (Disney character)

All I ate for lunch that day was _____ helpings of
(number)

_____. It was so _____. After lunch we waited in
(Disney park food)   (adjective)

line almost _____ hours to ride on _____. It scared
(number)   (Disney ride)

me so much, I just kept yelling, "_____!"
(exclamation)

I got soaking wet on that ride!

We stayed at the park until _____ at night. Just before we left,
(number)

_____ came up to me and gave me a _____ hug! I
(Disney character)   (adjective)

can't wait to go back again!

Acknowledgements

Thanks to everyone who submitted stories for this book. It was amazing to hear so many different stories about the Happiest Places on Earth. I only took one story from each person, but so many of you had terrific options to choose from. Thanks to Jill Williamson, my wife, who took time out of her life writing real novels to write up her story for me and proofreading this book. Find her outstanding books on Amazon and at JillWilliamson.com! Thanks to Becky Eisemann, who was one of the very first to submit her story. Thanks to Joe Torosian: Author of *Faith Views for Storm Riders*, *The Dead Bug Tales*, and *Tangent Dreams: A High School Football Novel* (All available on Amazon), who reluctantly gave me one of my favorite stories in this book. Thanks to Kim Titus who recruited her entire family to help with this project. Thanks to Andrew Long, a fellow Disney fanatic with his own Disney blog: WanderingInDisney.com.

Special thanks to Walt Disney,
whose legacy continues to inspire millions every day!

Keep 'em Coming!

This book is just the tip of the iceberg. There are so many more stories to share! If you have a Disney memory, I'd love to hear it! Did you meet a celebrity? Did you participate in a special event? Did something happen that seems almost unbelievable? You have a story to share with the world! I would love to put out a second volume of stories. I especially love the weird ones! Please submit your stories to:

BradWilliamsonWriter@gmail.com

Did you enjoy this book?

Post a review on Amazon!

Every review helps Disney fans find this book!

Join the Disney fun on Facebook

Facebook.com/groups/DisneyTriviaGames

Thanks for loving Disney as much as I do!

Watch for the next Brad Williamson book!

100 WORD
DISNEY
HISTORY

100 fascinating tales of Disney history told in bite-sized, 100-word nuggets

Did you know there is a Mt. Disney?
Do you remember Sam the Olympic Eagle?
Have you heard of the Disneyland pancake races?
YOU WILL!

COMINIG SOON!

SHADOW ANSWERS

Page 11	Hitchhiking Ghosts	The Haunted Mansion	Disneyland / Magic Kingdom
Page 18	The Orange Bird	Sunshine Tree Terrace	Magic Kingdom
Page 26	Sonny Eclipse	Cosmic Ray's Starlight Café	Magic Kingdom
Page 34	Dog	Pirates of the Caribbean	Disneyland / Magic Kingdom
Page 38	Caretaker	The Haunted Mansion	Disneyland / Magic Kingdom
Page 44	Lagoona Gator	Walk-Around Character	Typhoon Lagoon
Page 50	Big Al	The Country Bear Jamboree	Magic Kingdom
Page 56	Trader Sam	The Jungle Cruise	Magic Kingdom
Page 66	Duffy	Walk-Around Character	Tokyo DisneySea (and others)
Page 72	Redd (The Redhead)	Pirates of the Caribbean	Disneyland / Magic Kingdom
Page 82	Mickey Mouse	Walk-Around Character	All parks
Page 88	Albert the Monkey	Mystic Manor	Hong Kong Disneyland
Page 96	Ice Gator	Walk-Around Character	Blizzard Beach
Page 100	The Yeti (Harold)	Matterhorn Bobsleds	Disneyland
Page 104	Rex	Star Tours / Oga's Cantina	Disneyland / Hollywood Studios
Page 108	British Beefeater	it's a small world	Disneyland / Magic Kingdom
Page 116	Figment	Journey Into Imagination	Epcot
Page 120	Hatbox Ghost	The Haunted Mansion	Disneyland / Magic Kingdom
Page 126	Abraham Lincoln	Great Moments with Mr. Lincoln	Disneyland
Page 130	José	The Enchanted Tiki Room	Disneyland / Magic Kingdom

AWARD-WINNING FANTASY FROM JILL WILLIAMSON

Ladies and gentlemen,
boys and girls,
My Day at Disney
has now ended
its normal
operating day.

www.ingramcontent.com/pod-product-compliance
Lightning Source LLC
Chambersburg PA
CBHW020440290526
45785CB00002B/948